THE MILITARY HISTORY OF WORLD WAR II
Volume 2

EUROPEAN LAND BATTLES
1944-1945

*Supplies pour ashore as Allied troops move inland from the Normandy
beachhead.*

The Military History of World War II: Volume 2

EUROPEAN
LAND BATTLES
1944-1945

by Trevor Nevitt Dupuy

COL. U.S. ARMY, RET.

FRANKLIN WATTS, INC.
575 Lexington Avenue • New York 22

To George

PHOTO CREDITS

Frontispiece: OFFICIAL U.S. AIR FORCE PHOTO
Page 10: ACME PHOTO
*Pages 14, 16, 18, 19 (2), 20, 22, 23, 27, 29, 41, 43, 49, 52, 55, 58, 61,
64, 66, 67, 77* — WIDE WORLD PHOTOS
Pages 24, 32, 80: THREE LIONS
Page 37: IFF — FROM THREE LIONS
Pages 34, 50, 74: SIGNAL CORPS — FROM THREE LIONS

Contents

THE MILITARY HISTORY OF WORLD WAR II
Volume 2

EUROPEAN LAND BATTLES
1944-1945

EUROPE AT THE
BEGINNING OF 1944

AXIS-OCCUPIED TERRITORY
ALLIED-OCCUPIED TERRITORY
NEUTRAL COUNTRIES

Murmansk

NORWAY
Oslo
SWEDEN
FINLAND
Leningrad
JAN. 1944
FRONT LINE
NORTH
SEA
BALTIC SEA
Moscow
Smolensk
1941 RUSSIAN BORDER
ENGLAND
London
UNION OF SOVIET SOCIALIST REPUBLICS
ENGLISH CHANNEL
NETH.
BELG.
Berlin
Warsaw
Kiev
Dnieper R.
Charkov
NORMANDY
Paris
GERMANY
POLAND
FRANCE
SLOV.
Dniester R.
SWITZ.
Vienna
HUNGARY
Odessa
ITALY
YUGOSLAVIA
Danube R.
RUMANIA
PORTUGAL
SPAIN
Corsica
Rome
BULGARIA
BLACK SEA
Sardinia
Naples
GREECE
TURKEY
Sicily
MOROCCO
ALGERIA
MEDITERRANEAN SEA
Crete
Cyprus
IRAN
TUNISIA

Global Stalemate

By JANUARY 1, 1944, the Allies of World War II had stopped every important Axis attack in Europe, Asia and the Pacific. The Allied invasion of Italy in September, 1943, had caused the immediate downfall of the Italian dictator, Mussolini. There was no longer any chance that Germany or Japan could defeat the Allied "Big Three": the United States, Great Britain, and Soviet Russia. But the Allies could see no prospects of an early victory.

When Mussolini's Fascist government collapsed, Hitler's army had taken control of all of central and northern Italy, and had completely stopped the American and British advance a few miles north of Naples. In December of 1943 the Russians had made some minor gains in a new winter offensive, but the Germans were still firmly entrenched on Russian soil, and in the north their stranglehold on Leningrad was unshaken. In western Europe, Hitler's occupation forces were improving the already formidable defenses of the Atlantic Wall, that great line of German fortifications covering the North Sea coast from Norway to Belgium, then extending along the English Channel coast of France to Brittany, and southward to the border of Spain. There was no reason to think that the Allies would be able to shake the Nazis' iron grip on France, the Low Countries, Denmark, and Norway.

Meanwhile the Japanese had strengthened their hold on the richest regions of China and halted the Allied advance from India into Burma. General MacArthur was consolidating his gains on eastern New Guinea and the Solomon Islands, but the bulk of the vast area of the western Pacific was under firm Japanese control. Most Allied military men had resigned themselves to years of

1

SITUATION IN ASIA-PACIFIC

BEGINNING OF 1944

U.S.S.R. (Neutral)

OUTER MONGOLIA

SINKIANG

MANCHUKUO

JAPAN

PACIFIC OCEAN

Peiping

CHINA

TIBET

Tokyo

Chunking

Shanghai

BURMA ROAD

INDIA

FORMOSA

BURMA

WAKE I.

THAI-LAND

FR. INDO-CHINA

PHILIPPINE ISL.

MARSHALL ISL.

LEYTE

Singapore

INDIAN OCEAN

NETHERL. EAST INDIES

BISMARCK ARCHIPELAGO

SOLOMON ISL.

GILBERT ISL.

NEW GUINEA

GUADALCANAL

- - - JAPAN-OCCUPIED TERRITORY
NEUTRAL COUNTRIES
ALLIED-OCCUPIED TERRITORY

AUSTRALIA

tedious, costly attacks against islands made nearly impregnable by the industrious Japanese.

All in all, the war had just about reached a stalemate. The rulers of Germany and Japan had good reason to hope that the punishing losses they had already inflicted on the Allies would cause Americans, Britons, and Russians to make peace rather than fight on indefinitely with no clear prospect of victory.

2

Breaking the Deadlock in Europe

WHILE American, British, and other Allied troops were engaged in a grim, bloody struggle to keep the Germans occupied along the "Winter Line" in southern Italy, Allied leaders in the British Isles were preparing for the most gigantic military operation in all history.

In 1943 President Roosevelt of the United States and England's Prime Minister Churchill had approved the plan of the Combined Chiefs of Staff for a mighty land, sea, and air invasion of western Europe. This plan was given the name of Operation OVERLORD, and was scheduled to take place in May or June, 1944. To carry out OVERLORD, nearly 3,000,000 men would have to equipped, trained, and furnished with supplies. British and American military forces were already gathering in and around the British Isles. The whole area was alive with feverish but well-organized activity. Britain was becoming one huge military base.

The Allied military planners had carefully studied the coastline of German-held western Europe to find the best place to land an invading army. Among the many details that had to be considered was the exact moment of high and low tide at every landing beach from northern Norway to southern France. High tide was important. Then the landing craft could come closest to shore, and the attackers would not have to wade through so many of the underwater obstacles and mines the Germans had placed along the waterline. At the same time, the attackers would have less open beach to cross. They would be exposed for the least possible time to fire from German fortifications.

The day chosen for the landing must be one on which high tide came just at or shortly after daybreak. On such a day the landing craft could approach the coast under cover of darkness, but by the time the troops reached the beach, there would be light enough for them to see.

Before the landing was even attempted, however, the Allies must find the German forts and destroy them. Allied planners examined thousands of aerial photographs of the beach fortifications. From spies, from intercepted radio reports, and by aerial observation they learned a great deal about the locations and readiness of the German troops, and also about the number of airplanes, tanks, and guns, and the quantities of fuel, ammunition, and other supplies that Hitler had gathered in the west. From this information the Allied staff officers were able to calculate how many men they would need to defeat the defenders and meet possible German counterattacks on any of the possible beaches.

The Allied planners knew that they would have a limited number of landing craft, and that these craft could carry only a few divisions at one time. If the beach was far away from Britain, it would take the landing craft a long time to make the round trip. The build-up of Allied forces in the beachhead area would be slow. The Germans had concentrated their strongest defenses on the good beaches near Britain. But they were also ready to rush reinforcements to defend more distant beaches, and could do this more quickly by land than the Allies could by sea from Britain. Also, the more distant beaches could not be reached by the Allied fighter planes that must support the ground troops in their attack.

The Allied planners figured out how many forces — German and Allied — could be concentrated at any of the beaches within range of fighter planes based in Britain. Their calculations included the numbers of Allied troops that could be carried to the beaches in the available landing craft, the numbers of fighter planes that could fly from British bases to support the attacks, and the amounts of sup-

4

plies that could be ferried from England to the soldiers fighting on the beaches. They also figured the best ways for long-range British and American bombers to stop or slow down the arrival of German reinforcements.

Finally the Allied staff officers decided that the best place to make a landing would be the coast of Normandy in northern France. Here there would be the greatest chance for the Allied troops to gain a secure foothold.

To command all of the Allied forces that would make this great invasion, Roosevelt and Churchill had selected American General Dwight D. Eisenhower, who had been commanding Allied troops in North Africa, Sicily, and Southern Italy.

While the ground troops practiced for their landings with the combined Anglo-American naval force, the long-range Allied air forces were working methodically to weaken the German defenses and wipe the German air force from the skies. Early in 1944, the British Bomber Command and the American Strategic Air Forces in Europe had begun to shift the weight of their massive air assault from German war production to Hitler's defensive system in France. Now, slowly, the scales began to tip. The Luftwaffe's dwindling strength meant that General Eisenhower's soldiers would worry less about interference from the air when they landed on the Normandy beaches. It also meant that the Allied air forces could give the soldiers more help after the landing. They would be freer to attack German fortifications, troop concentrations, and supply lines.

By May, 1944, General Eisenhower reported to the Combined Chiefs of Staff that his soldiers, sailors, and airmen were ready for their dangerous invasion. The Combined Chiefs of Staff, with the approval of President Roosevelt and Prime Minister Churchill, ordered him to carry out Operation OVERLORD in June.

Steamroller in the East

IN 1941-42 and 1942-43, the Russians had proven that they were at their best as winter fighters. Since then, the Russians had so improved themselves and had built up such a tremendous army that they could outfight the weakened and outnumbered Germans in good weather, too. But winter warfare was still their specialty.

As 1943 turned into 1944, the Russians' renewed winter offensive, which had gotten off to a slow start, gathered momentum. Russian troops stormed across the frozen fringes of the great Pripet Marshes into eastern Poland to gain their first foothold outside the prewar boundaries of Russia.

Encouraged by this success, and by smaller gains along the main battle line in White Russia and the Ukraine, the Russians decided to make an all-out effort to end the two-year-long siege of Leningrad. Russian Prime Minister Josef Stalin secretly ordered Red Army reserves to northwest Russia. On January 15, the Soviet Army launched a surprise attack against the strong German siege lines that extended around three sides of Leningrad. The combination of surprise, of bitterly cold weather, and the overwhelming strength of the Russian assaults was too much for the Germans. In two weeks they fell back nearly a hundred miles. The siege of Leningrad had ended.

The Russian drive was now slowed by fierce German resistance, but during February the Red Army continued to forge ahead through snow, sleet, and ice. By the beginning of March they had advanced southwestward another hundred miles, right to the frontiers of prewar Estonia. Here they were finally halted by the concentration of all available German reserves, and by the difficulties of getting supplies and reinforcements to their most advanced troops.

Once again the Russians shifted their forces, this time to the southern part of the line where the Germans had weakened their

6

THE RUSSIAN FRONT

JANUARY-JUNE, 1944

FINLAND

L. Ladoga

Leningrad

ESTONIA

BALTIC SEA

LATVIA

Velikiye Luki

MOSCOW

LITHUANIA

Polotsk

EAST
PRUSSIA

Orsha

Smolensk

Minsk

Briansk

1941
RUSSIAN
BORDER

PRIPET MARSHES

Gomel

WARSAW

UNION OF SOVIET

POLAND

SOCIALIST

Przemysl

Lwow

Kiev

REPUBLICS

Tarnopol

Dnieper R.

Dniester R.

HUNGARY

U K R A I N E

Odessa

Perekop

Kerch

LINE, JANUARY 14

RUMANIA

CRIMEA

LINE, MARCH 1

Sevastopol

LINE, JUNE 22

USSR-CONTROLLED
IN JUNE 1944

Danube R.

0   100   200

Scale of Miles

BLACK SEA

7

defenses in order to send troops north. Early in March, the great Russian army groups caught the Germans off-balance and struck across a 400-mile front in the Ukraine. By the end of the month most of the Ukraine had been liberated, and Russian troops held all of southeastern Poland and northeastern Romania. The Russians were finally stopped only by the brilliant defensive tactics and fierce counterattacks of General Walther Model.

Because they could push no further on that front, the Russians shifted their forces once more. Again they caught the Germans off-balance. On April 8 they began an assault on the Crimean peninsula. While two Russian armies hammered their way across the Isthmus of Perekop, another army crossed the Strait of Kerch in an amphibious operation. The Germans were unable to stop the steady advance of these two columns, which met in the central Crimea in mid-April and continued down to Sevastopol. After a short siege, the Russians captured the city by assault on May 9.

The Germans now maintained only a few footholds in Russia proper. Hitler realized that Stalin's war machine was getting ready for another massive offensive during the summer, and insisted that his soldiers hold on at all costs. The German generals were doing everything in their power to get ready to meet the expected onslaught, but they knew they could not stop it unless they could withdraw to a new, fortified line. This Hitler would not allow them to do.

Overlord

AT THE BEGINNING of June, 1944, there were 58 German divisions occupying France, Belgium and Holland. More than half of these were weak coast defense or training divisions, while the remaining ten armored and 17 infantry divisions were under-strength and under-equipped. But these forces totaled about three-quarters of a million ground soldiers, many of them tough veterans of earlier German victories, and they were led by excellent officers. Hitler's Atlantic Wall gave them added strength. They were supported by German naval and air commands, but these had been greatly reduced in strength by the Allies' bombing attacks.

Field Marshal Gerd von Rundstedt was over-all commander of German forces in the West. Under him, Field Marshal Erwin Rommel commanded Army Group B in Holland, Belgium, and northern France. This was where the Germans expected an Allied invasion, so Rommel had been given more than two-thirds of the total German forces in the West. These forces were organized into the German Seventh Army, which occupied northwestern France, and the Fifteenth Army, which held northeastern France and the Low Countries.

Meanwhile, General Eisenhower's forces were getting ready for Operation OVERLORD, which was now scheduled to take place during the first week of June, 1944. British General Sir Bernard L. Montgomery commanded the Allied ground forces. Under him Lieutenant General Omar Bradley commanded the American First Army, and General Sir Miles Dempsey commanded the British Second Army. Forty-five divisions stood ready to take part in the invasion — nearly two-thirds of them American, the remainder British. With additional artillery, tank and engineer units, they totaled about

American soldiers about to board landing craft as D-Day comes closer.

1,000,000 fighting men. Nearly 1,000,000 more soldiers were ready to provide supplies and ammunition, to take care of sick and wounded, to drive trucks, to repair equipment, to operate radios and telephones, and to do other important tasks. Without these "support elements," the front-line soldiers could not keep fighting even for a day.

Almost another million men comprised the naval and air forces taking part in Operation OVERLORD. The Anglo-American naval force was commanded by British Admiral Sir Bertram Ramsey. His duty was to control and to protect the ships and landing craft that carried the soldiers to Normandy, while his battleships, cruisers, and destroyers hammered the German defenses with their big guns.

The supporting air forces were divided into two groups. The long-range American bombers, commanded by American General Carl Spaatz, were placed under General Eisenhower's command for only a short period just before and just after the attack. As soon as the army had a firm foothold in northern France, these big aircraft would be sent back to their job of smashing German war industry. The British and American tactical air forces, under British Air Marshal Sir Trafford Leigh-Mallory, would continue to provide close air support of the fighting troops.

Although the Allies had about twice as many ground troops as Rundstedt and Rommel, Allied success was not certain. In the first place, by using every available landing craft and transport airplane, the Allies could put less than nine divisions ashore on the first day of the assault. For the next week or more, the overworked Allied landing craft could put only one division a day on the beaches, in addition to the ammunition, food and other supplies needed by the fighting men already ashore. These troops would not have their full amounts of supporting artillery. Until they moved inland far enough to construct airfields near the beaches, they would have only scanty air support from short-range fighter planes based in southern Britain. The guns of the supporting naval vessels would make up for some of the lack of artillery and air support, but not for all of it. It was most important for the attackers to capture a seaport, where troops and supplies could be unloaded more quickly and efficiently than over the beaches.

General Eisenhower and his planners were worried about three things: first, if the Germans could gather twenty or more divisions

11

to strike the Allied beachhead during the first few days, they might be able to push the invaders into the sea; second, if the weather should be bad, it might be impossible to transport enough troops and supplies to reinforce the beachhead (this would give the Germans more time to bring up reinforcements, and make it easier for them to counterattack); third, if the Germans learned about the attack in advance, they might be able to concentrate troops near the landing area, or to destroy large numbers of landing craft carrying troops or supplies. Then the whole plan might fail right at the outset, and thousands of Allied soldiers would be killed without accomplishing anything.

Trouble began even before the assault got under way. D-Day — the day scheduled for the landing — was to be June 5. Troops were loading on their vessels when a storm sprang up on the English Channel. The weather experts forecasted several days of bad weather, but said that there would be one relatively calm day — June 6.

General Eisenhower knew that the troops could not land on the fifth, and that if they landed on the sixth, he could not give them all the supplies and reinforcements they needed for the next few days. But if the assault was delayed, the tides would change and the troops would not be able to land at dawn. It would be too dangerous to make the landing in the middle of the day, when the Germans could see the boats approaching. It would be equally dangerous to make it in the middle of the night, when the attackers could not see where they were going. Furthermore, a delay of even a few days would mean that the Germans might discover the whole plan, and then success might never be possible.

Eisenhower took a chance and ordered the attack to go ahead, one day later than scheduled. D-Day was now set for June 6, 1944.

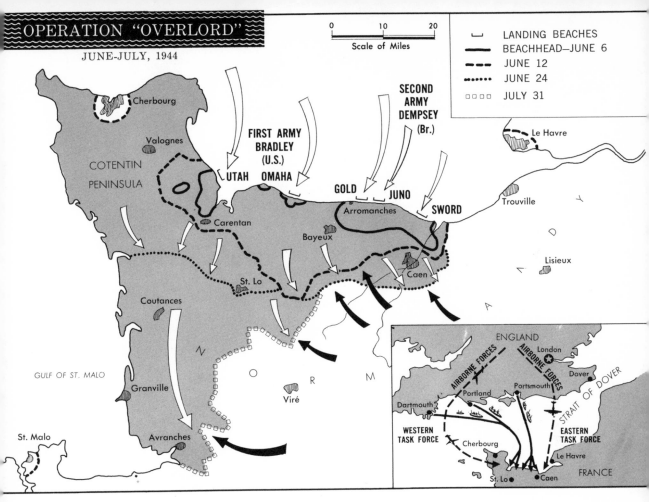

OPERATION "OVERLORD"

JUNE-JULY, 1944

Scale of Miles
0   10   20

	LANDING BEACHES
	BEACHHEAD—JUNE 6
	JUNE 12
	JUNE 24
	JULY 31

Cherbourg

Valognes

COTENTIN
PENINSULA

FIRST ARMY
BRADLEY
(U.S.)

UTAH OMAHA

SECOND
ARMY
DEMPSEY
(Br.)

Le Havre

GOLD JUNO

SWORD

Arromanches

Trouville

Carentan

Bayeux

Lisieux

St. Lo

Caen

Coutances

N

GULF OF ST. MALO

O   R   M

Granville

Viré

St. Malo

Avranches

ENGLAND

AIRBORNE FORCES

London

AIRBORNE FORCES

Dover

STRAIT OF DOVER

Portland

Portsmouth

Dartmouth

WESTERN
TASK FORCE

Cherbourg

EASTERN
TASK FORCE

Le Havre

St. Lo   Caen

FRANCE

D-Day

BEGINNING AT 2:00 A.M. on June 6, American paratroopers began to
land just behind the German coastal defenses in northern Normandy. An hour later, Allied planes began an intense aerial bombardment of the beach fortifications. At sunrise the big guns of
American and British naval vessels began to smash the forts. Less
than an hour later — at 6:30 A.M. — the first waves of assault infantry
and tanks were landed on the beaches. Right behind them came
another wave, and another and another, all through that long, ter-

rible day. They kept coming just as fast as the Navy crews of the landing craft could turn around to go back to the waiting ships offshore and pick up more soldiers, tanks, guns, and supplies.

Meanwhile, the Allied troops already reaching shore were finding that the German defenses were tough. First there were bands of underwater obstacles. Some of the landing craft foundered on these, others were blown up by mines just under water at the shoreline. The beaches themselves were covered with barbed wire, while land mines were strewn all around, just under the sand. Many of the concrete forts and machine-gun emplacements behind the beaches had been knocked out, but some were still full of fight. They began to send withering streams of bullets sweeping over the sand. In some places the attackers managed to crawl or run past these beach de-

American troops wade through the surf to the Normandy shore.

fenses only to find anti-tank walls and ditches, more mine fields, and more barbed wire. Further inland, German mortars and artillery began to fire along the water's edge, and at those places where the Allied soldiers were gathering.

British and American losses were terribly heavy. It seemed impossible for men to survive and fight under the appalling conditions that now existed on the beaches. But in fact, the Allied plans were going as well as had been expected. The troops had known what they would find, and they had been trained to work their way around the beach defenses and fortifications. They called on the supporting naval vessels to shoot at the German gun emplacements. Allied fighter planes swept across the English Channel to dive-bomb the most stubborn defenders and then to strafe them with machine-gun fire. The planes then returned to Britain to get more fuel, more bombs, and more bullets for another run back to help the ground soldiers.

The advance preparations had worked out well. The Allied naval and aerial bombardment of the defenses had been so intense that even when the forts had survived, the German soldiers inside them were still groggy when the first wave of Allied troops hit the beach; the defending fire was neither as accurate nor as heavy as it would otherwise have been. Meanwhile, the airborne troops had concentrated in small groups and begun to attack the German defenses from the rear and harass the German artillery.

By nightfall of June 6, the British attackers on the east had established a beachhead nearly 20 miles long and about five miles deep; they had pushed to the outskirts of the city of Caen. On the west, at "Utah" Beach, the American VII Corps held an area almost ten miles wide, with spearheads more than four miles inland. Only in the center, at the American "Omaha" Beach, had there been

Trucks move over portable harbor, or "Mulberry," to Omaha Beach on the Normandy coast.

really serious trouble. Here frowning cliffs overlooked narrow beaches, and the German defenders were unexpectedly numerous. The American V Corps, however, managed to seize two narrow strips of beach and cliff. It held on to them through the day and into the night. Then, as reinforcements came ashore, the attackers pushed out again.

The Allies were now advancing at all the beachheads. Their initial footholds were secure. But could they stand up under the expected German counterattacks?

Build-up on the Beaches

IN THEIR painstaking preparations for the attack, the Allied planners had figured every conceivable way of getting the greatest pos-

16

sible number of men and supplies onto the beaches in the shortest possible time. They had even carried out British Prime Minister Winston Churchill's suggestion of building artificial harbors to speed up the unloading and protect the beach landing areas from the pounding surf. Right after D-Day, they towed from England several old ships and a number of specially built concrete barges. They sunk these near the beaches in such a way as to make breakwaters and docks.

There were two of these artificial harbors, one at Omaha Beach for the American area, the other near Arromanches for the British. MULBERRY was the code name for this secret plan, and so the two harbors were called "Mulberries."

The Mulberries played an important part in the feverish race between the Allies and the Germans to build up forces in the beachhead area. The Allies had a great disadvantage in this race. As the weather experts had predicted, a number of storms swept through the English Channel during the week after D-Day, seriously slowing up the movement of men and supplies to the beachheads. One of these storms completely wrecked the American Mulberry at Omaha Beach. Fortunately, the British Mulberry survived the storm. Both armies used it constantly for several months.

The Germans, too, were having serious troubles. In the first place, Allied planes swept continuously over northern France and prevented the Germans from moving during the day. Secondly, the secretly organized French Resistance Forces, having learned that the Allies had landed, rose against the Germans. The Resistance Forces blew up bridges, railroad lines, trains, and trucks, making it difficult for the Germans to move men or supplies. Finally, Hitler had been fooled completely by a pretended Allied attack against German defense further northeast, opposite the narrow Strait of

Landing craft shuttle supplies over a Normandy beach to Allied troops fighting inland.

Dover. For more than six weeks he kept almost half of German Army Group B in northeast France, waiting for an attack that never came.

By June 12, the build-up in Normandy had reached the point where both sides realized that the Allies could no longer be driven back into the sea. But the Germans had built a chain of entrenchments and fortifications around the beachhead, and reinforcements

Diesel railroad engines are landed on the Normandy beach to carry supplies inland.

Fresh equipment for Allied troops in Normandy.

were now arriving from Germany and elsewhere in France. OVER-LORD had succeeded, but would the Allies be able to push their way out of Normandy?

Operation Cobra

ONCE the Normandy beachhead was secure, General Eisenhower and his subordinates began to prepare for a blow that would shatter

British Commandos (lower right) seek cover from enemy snipers in Normandy.

the strengthening German defense in Normandy. The first step would be to capture the French seaport of Cherbourg so that troops and supplies could be brought into the beachhead area more quickly.

Major General J. Lawton Collins' American VII Corps began to attack westward and northward from the Utah Beach area on June 14. By June 18, they had cut their way across the Cotentin Peninsula, cutting off the troops in Cherbourg from the rest of the German army. Two days later, they had reached the outskirts of Cherbourg. That seaport had been strongly fortified by the Germans, however, and the Germans refused an American demand to surrender. Now General Collins, with the assistance of overwhelming air support, hurled three divisions against the fortifications. On June 27, the Germans surrendered, but before they gave up, they thoroughly destroyed the docks and unloading equipment.

Until August 7, the Allies were unable to use the port of Cherbourg. But by means of the remaining Mulberry and improvised measures on the beaches, the American and British engineers and supply men managed to pour great quantities of men and equipment into the crowded beachhead.

Meanwhile, the Allies were working up a plan that they hoped would smash through the German lines. It was called Operation COBRA. It was a good name, because the build-up of Allied troops in the beachhead was just like the coiling of a snake as it prepares to strike.

As General Montgomery visualized it, Operation COBRA would consist of four parts. At the start, the American First and British Second armies would push a little farther into Normandy to make more room for the coiling snake. Along the beaches, Lieutenant General George S. Patton would collect his newly organized Third American Army. Then the British troops on the east would do all

*American infantry-
men duck behind a
hedgerow as German
shells burst overhead.*

they could to attract German reserves to that part of the line. Next, General Bradley's First Army would punch a hole through the German line further west. Patton's army would be the cobra's head, darting through the gap to strike deep behind the German lines.

The Americans and the British soon had trouble setting the stage for Operation COBRA. The Germans were making such good use of the "hedgerows" of Normandy that it was almost impossible for the Allies to advance. The Normandy hedgerows are quite unlike the hedges in America. They are long mounds of earth, several yards thick and usually about six feet high, filled with the thick, gnarled roots of the tangled thickets of ancient trees and shrubs that grow on top of the mounds. These hedgerows surrounded every little field, and lined all of the roads. They were ready-made fortresses for the Germans.

And so the first stage of Operation COBRA went slowly. But as the Allies built up their strength, they found ways to deal with the hedgerows. One of the best devices — invented by a bright young American tank soldier — was a steel horn bolted to the front of a tank. This would dig into a hedgerow like a bulldozer, while bullets glanced harmlessly off the tank's armor. At the same time, Allied

Bomb-battered railroad station at Cherbourg, France.

German prisoners are marched through Cherbourg.

infantry soldiers learned how to fight their way through the hedge-rows with the fewest possible losses.

After the Germans had stopped several British attacks at Caen, General Montgomery ordered his troops to make another more powerful assault. This would start the second phase of Operation COBRA. The British began their advance on July 17. Three days later, after they captured Caen, the advance was halted. The Germans had shifted all of their reserves to the eastern end of the Allied line, just as Montgomery had hoped.

Now came General Bradley's great attack. It was preceded by a tremendous air "carpet" bombing attack by all of the long-range heavy bombers of the American and British strategic air forces. Then the American VII Corps spearheaded a drive southward, just west of the town of St. Lo. By July 31, after an advance of 40 miles, the Americans had passed the town of Avranches at the base of the Cotentin Peninsula. It was time for the "cobra" to strike.

Breakout

ON AUGUST 1, the newly created American Third Army swept through the narrow gap at Avranches. It headed south and southwest to reach the mouth of the Loire River and cut off the Brittany Peninsula. With magnificent air support, and under the driving, brilliant leadership of Patton, the troops swept ahead. By August 6 they had reached the Atlantic Ocean north of St. Nazaire. By August 13, they held the entire line of the Loire River from St. Nazaire to Angers.

But the Germans, who had introduced *blitzkrieg* to the world, did not intend to give up so easily. Rommel had been seriously wounded by an American air attack, but his place had been taken by Field Marshal Gunther von Kluge. Von Kluge was a competent soldier, and a man who refused to panic. Gathering all of his armored divisions, including some recently arrived reinforcements, he mounted an intensive attack against Avranches on August 6. If it succeeded, it would cut off Patton's spearheads, and possibly spell disaster for the Allied armies. For two days the situation was desperate. The German stormed Avranches, and the Americans barely held them off.

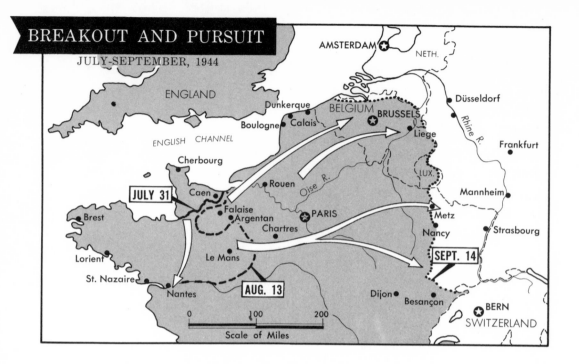

ENGLAND

AMSTERDAM

NETH.

Düsseldorf

Dunkerque

BELGIUM

BRUSSELS

Liege

Rhine R.

Frankfurt

Boulogne

Calais

ENGLISH CHANNEL

Cherbourg

Rouen

Oise R.

LUX.

Mannheim

JULY 31

Caen

Falaise

Argentan

PARIS

Chartres

Metz

Nancy

Strasbourg

SEPT. 14

Brest

Lorient

Le Mans

AUG. 13

St. Nazaire

Nantes

Dijon

Besançon

BERN

SWITZERLAND

0   100   200

Scale of Miles

Then General Bradley — who now commanded the 12th Army Group, including the First and Third American armies — threw additional divisions into the line. They slowed, then stopped, von Kluge's attack. Montgomery's new British 21st Army Group — consisting of the British Second and Canadian First armies — also stepped up its assaults below Caen, forcing von Kluge to divert forces from his main attack.

Suddenly the picture changed; Patton, having reached the Loire, began to sweep northeastward. Spearheads of the Third Army approached Argentan from the south, while the Canadian First Army pushed down toward Falaise. Most of German Army Group B was further west, where it was in danger of being completely surrounded.

With the same coolness he had shown when he prepared for his attack against Avranches, Kluge stopped his assaults and began to withdraw rapidly to the east. Meanwhile, he threw every available unit into the fight to prevent the Allied jaws from closing at Falaise and Argentan. The situation had changed so quickly that both Bradley and Montgomery were afraid the American Third and Canadian First armies would attack each other by mistake. They ordered both advances to stop, then issued new orders that would avoid confusion.

The Allied halt lasted only one day, but it enabled Kluge to get a large part of his army out of the trap. Many Allied officers thought it had been a mistake to permit this, but even so, 100,000 Germans

Armored vehicles west of Caen. On the right is a "flail tank," used for exploding mines.

had been captured, and the remnants streaming east, hammered by aerial bombardment, were in confusion.

It is really doubtful if the Allied success could have been much more complete. In the fighting in Normandy the Germans had lost more than 500,000 men. Two German armies had for all practical purposes ceased to exist. Allied losses had been less than half as great.

Pursuit

As THE demoralized Germans fled east, the Allies pursued them, cutting off stragglers and slicing through any German units that attempted to stand and fight. On August 26, Patton's Third Army led the way across the Seine on the right flank of the Allied armies. Just to his left the American First Army, now under Lieutenant General Courtney H. Hodges, crossed the river on both sides of Paris. The French 2nd Armored Division, attached to Hodges' army, was given the honor of reoccupying the French capital. On the left, the two armies of Montgomery's 21st Army Group drove northeastward along the coastal plain toward Belgium.

Hoping to capture the seaports of Belgium and Holland, and then to overrun the industrial Ruhr region of northern Germany, General Eisenhower ordered that most of the dwindling Allied supplies should be given to the British 21st Army Group. What little was left was to go to the American First Army. This meant that Patton's American Third Army— racing across east-central France — had to get along with the small amounts of food, fuel, and ammunition they carried with them.

Hitler and his generals realized that the Allies had limited supplies in Normandy, and that these would soon be used up. It would

Smoke from burning German equipment clouds the road as Allied infantrymen and armor move toward Falaise, France.

be impossible to bring enough supplies over the Normandy beaches and through Cherbourg to furnish the great Allied armies. Therefore, the retreating Germans left behind them strong garrisons to hold the main seaports. Hitler felt that if the Allied armies failed to receive supplies through these ports, they must stop their advance.

And stop they did. Patton's army ground to a halt on August 30, just east of the Meuse River. The other three armies were forced to stop early in September, when they ran out of fuel for tanks and trucks. By this time the Allies had reached the German border. They held most of Belgium and Luxembourg, and all of northern France as far east as the line of the Moselle River. General Patton was sure that he could have pushed right on through the Siegfried Line if he had had enough gasoline, and he thought the war could have been over before the end of 1944.

As we shall see, when the Allies finally got started again, the Germans fought bitterly and bravely to defend their country. It is doubtful if the war could have ended in 1944 under any circumstances. But that it would end in an Allied victory, no one could now doubt. The question was, when would it end, and how?

Southern France

Operation ANVIL

THE GERMAN collapse in northern France had been hastened and assisted by a dramatic Allied blow to the south. On August 15 the American Seventh Army, commanded by Lieutenant General Alexander M. Patch, carried out Operation ANVIL, an amphibious landing on the coast of the French Riviera, about midway between the cities of Nice and Toulon. This army had been convoyed through the Mediterranean to the French coast by an Allied naval task force commanded by American Vice-Admiral Henry K. Hewitt.

The Seventh Army was composed of American and Free French forces, plus a few British units. The actual assault landing was made by the American VI Corps, commanded by Major General Lucian K. Truscott. This corps consisted of three American divisions, an Anglo-American airborne task force (slightly smaller than a division), a few small French units, and a unit of tough Canadian-American Rangers and Commandos. The four divisions of the French I and II Corps, which had not been trained for an amphibious assault, remained in their ships offshore. They would come in as reserves after the beachhead was secure.

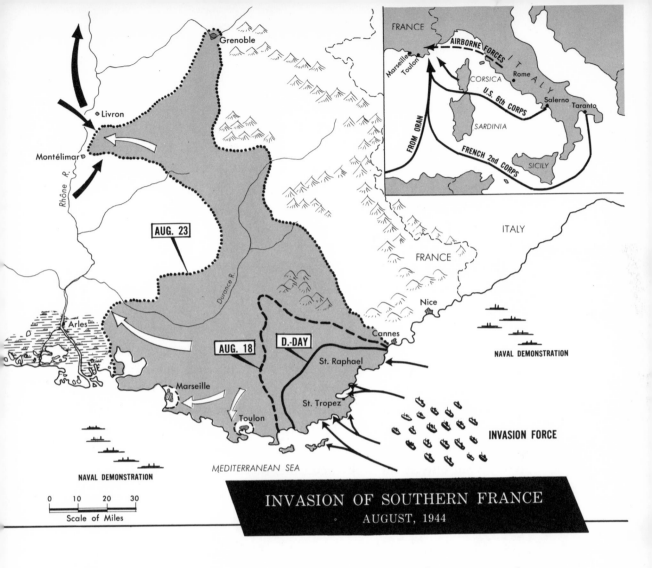

INVASION OF SOUTHERN FRANCE
AUGUST, 1944

The German garrison of southern France was the Nineteenth Army, consisting of seven understrength infantry divisions and one armored division, under the command of General Wiese. The Germans were caught completely by surprise. They had thought the invasion convoy was heading for northern Italy to take part in the bitter conflict still being waged on that peninsula.

31

The dawn landing on August 15 was a success. The well-trained Americans hit the beach in excellent weather, and the German defenders who had survived the preliminary aerial and naval bombardments were too stunned to offer serious opposition. To add to the German difficulties, just before dawn the Anglo-American airborne task force had made a perfect landing on top of a German corps headquarters. They created such confusion that the local commander could not coordinate the action of his troops.

The original Allied plan had been to capture the two large seaports of Marseille and Toulon as rapidly as possible, then to drive the Germans northward up the Rhone River Valley. Until those ports were captured, or until large supplies had been built up on the beaches, it would have been dangerous to try any large-scale advance. But the German Nineteenth Army had been badly shattered in the first assaults. By evening of August 17 — after only two days of fighting — the VI Corps had completely broken through the coastal defense, and the French follow-up troops were coming ashore, a full day earlier than had been planned. General Truscott now made one of the bold decisions of the war.

Flying Fortresses hit German-held aqueduct near Cannes, southern France.

Race to Montelimar

WITH General Patch's approval, Truscott decided that the French divisions could attack Toulon and Marseille while he, with his American corps, struck directly northwestward across the difficult mountains of southeastern France. If his troops could move fast enough, and could take enough of their guns and heavy equipment with them, they might cut off the retreat of the entire German Nineteenth Army. The difficulty, of course, was the fact that only a few of the trucks and tanks of the Allied divisions had come ashore, and there had not been time to collect a reserve supply of fuel or ammunition on the beaches.

The shattered Germans, meanwhile, were retreating as fast as they could to the Rhone Valley, knowing that this was their only way of escape to northern France and to Germany. At Hitler's orders, General Wiese left a division to hold Toulon and another to defend Marseille. These Germans were ordered to hold out as long as possible in order to delay the Allied build-up of supplies. The remainder of the Nineteenth Army — about 100,000 men — hurried north before Truscott's VI Corps could encircle them.

Truscott sent one division to pursue directly behind the retreating Germans, while a small armored task force and the other two divisions moved as rapidly as possible through the mountains further east. On August 21 the spearheads of this encircling force reached the hills overlooking the Rhone Valley near the town of Montelimar. At about the same time the leading elements of the retreating German Nineteenth Army were approaching Montelimar from the south.

For six days the Americans and Germans struggled for control of the Rhone Valley near Montelimar. Both fought under difficult

Montelimar, France. Girls convicted of fraternizing with the enemy are marched through the town before having their heads shaved.

handicaps. The Americans, at the end of a long, roundabout supply line, with few trucks and fewer airplanes, were constantly short of ammunition, gasoline, food, and all other kinds of supplies. The Germans were in headlong retreat; their spirits were low, they were unprepared for battle, and were too disorganized to fight efficiently. They, too, were short of supplies, but they were better off for ammunition and gasoline than the Americans.

While some of the Germans kept the Americans busy on the east bank of the river, others crossed over to escape northward on side

34

roads. Occasionally the American attacks actually reached the banks of the Rhone, but each time the Germans counterattacked successfully.

Finally, by August 28, all three American divisions had concentrated near Montelimar, and in a determined effort they completely closed the Rhone Valley. The battle was over. About 15,000 Germans surrendered near Montelimar; nearly 50,000 more were captured at Marseille, Toulon, and in the valley south of the American roadblock. Barely half of the German Nineteenth Army escaped; it had been ruined as a fighting organization.

Truscott and his men pursued the fleeing Germans without a pause for rest. On September 11 the leading elements of the south France invasion force made contact with the right flank of Patton's Third Army near Dijon. The Allied front now extended unbroken from Switzerland to the North Sea.

Russian Summer Offensives of 1944

Poland and the Baltic

EARLY IN 1944 the German General Staff warned Hitler that his armies on the Russian front were spread dangerously thin. Germany had been unable to replace all the losses of the three previous terrible years of fighting, while the Russian army had grown enormously in numbers and had improved greatly in fighting qualities. The German staff officers wanted to withdraw to a line extending from Riga in Latvia to Lvov in southern Poland, and then southeastward behind the Dniester River to the Black Sea. This front would have been only two-thirds as long as that which the Germans

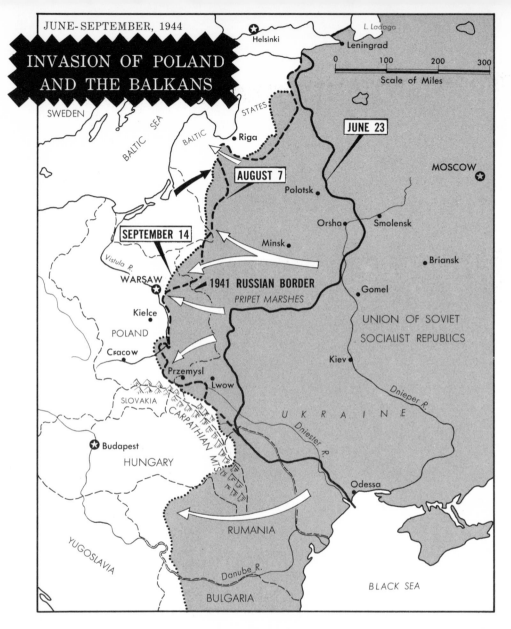

JUNE-SEPTEMBER, 1944

INVASION OF POLAND AND THE BALKANS

SWEDEN

BALTIC SEA

STATES

BALTIC

Riga

L. Ladoga

Leningrad

0   100   200   300
Scale of Miles

JUNE 23

MOSCOW

AUGUST 7

Polotsk

Orsha   Smolensk

Minsk

Briansk

SEPTEMBER 14

Vistula R.

WARSAW

1941 RUSSIAN BORDER

Gomel

PRIPET MARSHES

Kielce

POLAND

UNION OF SOVIET

SOCIALIST REPUBLICS

Cracow

Kiev

Przemysl

Lwow

SLOVAKIA

U K R A I N E

Dnieper R.

CARPATHIAN MTS.

Dniester R.

Budapest

HUNGARY

Odessa

RUMANIA

YUGOSLAVIA

Danube R.

BLACK SEA

BULGARIA

held in April. The German staff officers believed that by strongly
fortifying this shortened line they could stop the Russians indefinitely.

Hitler refused to listen. He had already dismissed his best field

36

commander in the east, Marshal von Manstein, because he had made this same suggestion. Now Hitler insisted his armies must hold on to every inch of Russian territory they occupied. Instead of building deep defensive zones, as his generals suggested, he threw most of the German reserve forces into the front lines, with orders to hold on at all costs. He collected the few remaining reserves in southern Poland, because he expected the next Russian attack to come between the Pripet Marshes and the Carpathian Mountains.

Warsaw, Poland. Germans clear the rubble from a bombed-out house.

Instead, late in June, the Russians struck north of the Pripet Marshes. In ten days they overran 25 German divisions and blasted a hole 250 miles wide and 250 miles deep in the German lines. It was the worst defeat Germany had yet suffered in the war, and it was all due to Hitler's stubborn refusal to take the advice of his military experts.

Now that it was almost too late, Hitler called on General Walther Model to take command of the shattered Central Army Group of the German army. Model worked a miracle, much as Marshal Manstein had done a year before. He scraped together the few remaining reserves, withdrew troops from all other parts of the front, and built a new German line just east of Warsaw. In violent counterattacks he slowed the Russian advance in eastern Poland and finally, in early August, halted the Russians on the banks of the Vistula, in sight of Warsaw.

Meanwhile, the Russians had also been attacking in the Baltic States. Though the outnumbered Germans fought stubbornly, they were unable to halt the steady Russian advances. But the attackers became exhausted, and their supplies could not keep up with the advance. By early August the line was stabilized near Riga.

The Plot to Assassinate Hitler

On July 20, at the height of this terrible, bloody fighting, Hitler paid one of his frequent visits to the Eastern Front headquarters in East Prussia. There one of his staff officers, Lieutenant Colonel Claus von Stauffenberg, tried to kill him by exploding a bomb concealed in a briefcase near his chair.

Stauffenberg was one of a group of German officers who had conspired to end Hitler's tyrannical and disastrous rule over Germany.

These men were disgusted by Hitler's gangster methods and by his mass-murders of the Jewish people. But most of all they were aware of the terrible losses of German soldiers. They knew that Hitler's refusal to listen to military advice would mean the ruin of Germany. They had planned to kill him, to seize control of the government, and to make peace with the Allies. The explosion of the bomb was to be the signal for the uprising.

By chance, Hitler left his chair just before the bomb exploded. At the moment of the blast he was partly protected by a table and some other furniture. He was badly injured, but he lived, and immediately gave orders to put down the conspiracy. The plotters were seized and cruelly tortured before they were put to death. Field Marshal Rommel, who was in the plot, was allowed to commit suicide instead of being tortured and shot.

After this attempt on his life, Hitler imposed an even more ruthless control over Germany. He had always been suspicious of his generals; now he became even more so.

The Tragedy of Warsaw

WHILE Hitler was stamping out the military plot against him, a quite different kind of uprising was taking place in his crumbling German empire. At Warsaw, early in August, the Polish people had been given new hope by the approach of the Russians. Under the leadership of Polish General Bor-Komorowski, the Poles had secretly organized, collected weapons, and prepared to rise against the Germans when they thought the time was ripe. When they heard the Russian guns and saw the smoke of battle to the southeast, they struck.

Once they had recovered from their surprise, the Germans reacted strongly. While Model held the Russians off to the east, other German army units and the SS Storm Troopers of Gestapo leader Heinrich Himmler attacked the Polish patriots. Fortressed in the ruined buildings of Warsaw, the Poles fought bravely, but the Germans cruelly suppressed the revolt in a few weeks of hard street fighting.

Surprisingly the Russians — who were now in sight of Warsaw — made no effort to help the insurrectionists. The heroic, unfortunate Poles soon learned why. They were still loyal to the old government that had fled to England after Poland's defeat by Germany in 1939. Since then, Stalin had set up a puppet "government" composed of Polish Communist refugees. He wanted to get rid of all the Poles who were loyal to the old government, and he had decided to let the Germans do it for him before he tried to capture Warsaw. Few countries have ever been treated so cruelly as was Poland in the terrible years from 1939 to 1945.

The Balkans

LEAVING the Polish patriots to the mercies of Hitler's Nazis, Stalin concentrated his forces further south. He wanted to conquer the Balkans before the British and Americans thought about that part of the world.

On August 20 the Russians mounted another tremendous offensive, this time in Romania. As the Germans tried to stem the advance, the Romanian army suddenly deserted them and joined the Russians. Sixteen German divisions were cut off, and almost all were killed or captured.

Soon after this, the Bulgarians, too, deserted the Germans. With hardly any opposition left in front of them, the Russians swept

A bombed German oil train burns as British troops enter a German village.

through Romania and Bulgaria. Stalin immediately set up a new government in Bulgaria, and on September 8, that country declared war against Germany.

General Heinz Guderian now became Hitler's Chief of Staff, and was in direct control of operations on the Eastern Front. Scraping up reinforcements from Germany and from other parts of the front, he built a new line in the Transylvanian Mountains of western Romania and in the Balkan Mountains in western Bulgaria. For a time, at least, the Russian offensives were brought to a halt.

End of the War in Finland

WHEN FINLAND joined Germany in the war against Russia in 1941, it had merely wanted to regain the territory lost to Russia during the "Winter War" of 1940-41. Once they had done this, the Finns held a line north of Leningrad and then stopped active operations.

In 1942, with the help of Britain and America, the Finns had tried to make peace with Russia. Stalin had refused, and in June of 1944 he made another big attack on Finland. As they had three years earlier, the Finns fought bravely and well; the powerful Russian armies advanced very slowly. Meanwhile, both sides began to negotiate to make peace. The war in Finland ended on September 4, 1944, on almost exactly the same terms as had been established at the end of the Winter War, though this time Finland was forced to pay an indemnity to Russia and to give up some additional territory.

Into the Siegfried Line

Pause at the Frontier of Germany

BY MID-SEPTEMBER, 1944, the Western Allies had liberated most of the German-occupied areas of western Europe except the Netherlands and scattered regions in Belgium and France. The main battle line was anchored on the North Sea near Ostend and extended east to include Antwerp and most of Belgium. Near Aachen, American troops held a tiny portion of the Siegfried Line, actually on German soil. From here the Allied battle line ran generally southward to include most of Luxembourg, then followed the general line of the Moselle River through eastern France to the border of Switzerland.

An elderly German tends his potato crop in a patch of ground before his ruined house in the border city of Aachen.

There were pockets of German troops holding several coastal areas in France: in Brittany, on the Bay of Biscay, and along the English Channel.

After the successful Allied landings in Normandy in June, Hitler had dismissed von Rundstedt from his command of German armies in the west. But following the breakout from the beachhead, the German dictator had recalled von Rundstedt. He had also shifted Model from the Russian Front to take command of Army Group B on the northern portion of the Western Front. Further south, General Hermann Balck commanded Army Group G. When the Allied troops ran out of supplies, these three men had taken advantage of the Allied delay to organize an effective defensive line. Model's Army Group B, with three armies, extended from the North Sea to

43

the Moselle River; Balck, with three armies, held the rest of the front to Switzerland. Together they had 63 divisions, but these were only at about half-strength.

On the Allied side, British Field Marshal Montgomery's 21st Army Group — General H. D. G. Crerar's First Canadian Army and General Dempsey's British Second Army — held the front from the North Sea to the Meuse River near Maastrich, Holland. Most of the remainder of the line was held by American General Bradley's 12th Army Group, consisting of the large American First and Third armies under Generals Hodges and Patton. The southeast section of the Allied line was commanded by American General Jacob Devers, whose newly created 6th Army Group included two small armies: General Patch's American Seventh and the French First under General De Lattre de Tassigny. The new American Ninth Army, commanded by General William H. Simpson, was operating against the German-held coastal regions of western France.

General Eisenhower knew that he could not start another big offensive until he could get more supplies to his front-line troops. Food, ammunition, and other equipment were pouring across the beaches in Normandy, through the rebuilt port of Cherbourg, and into the ports of Toulon and Marseille in Southern France. But then these supplies had to be brought to the front by truck or by the badly damaged French railroads. As more and more Allied divisions arrived in France, Eisenhower found that he did not have enough supplies and that he could not get what he had to the front fast enough. He decided that the most important thing for Allied forces to do, therefore, was to repair the great damaged port of Antwerp, in Belgium, so that he could bring most of his supplies in through that city.

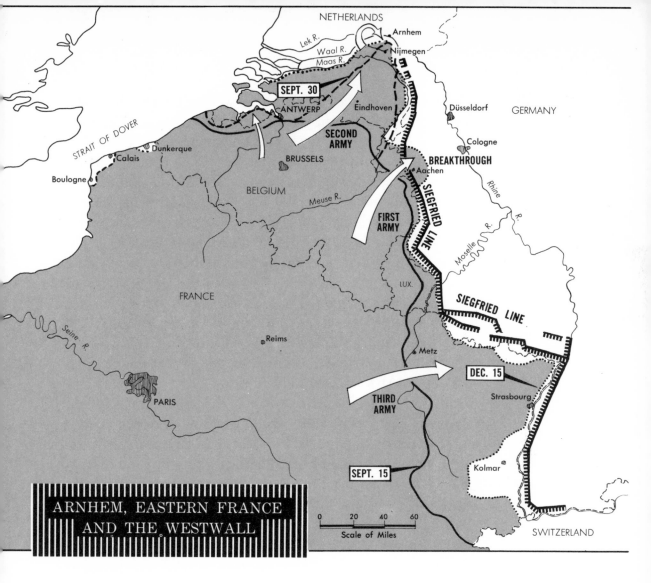

ARNHEM, EASTERN FRANCE AND THE WESTWALL

Antwerp and Arnhem

ANTWERP was on the broad Scheldt River, nearly 50 miles inland from the North Sea. British troops had captured the city early in September, but the Germans still held most of the lower Scheldt

River in Belgium and southern Holland, as well as the Dutch coastal islands that overlooked the entrance to the ship channel. The Germans knew that as long as they controlled these areas the Allies would be unable to use Antwerp as a seaport. They decided, therefore to hold on to their positions along the Scheldt as long as possible. Their job was made easier by the network of canals in the region. It was easy for them to defend the waterways and their dikes, but Allied tanks were useless in such country.

Eisenhower decided that most of the supplies that were reaching the front should be used in an attempt to clear the Germans out of the positions blocking Antwerp. So the American troops further south had to stay quietly in their positions while Montgomery and his British troops went ahead with this difficult job. With Eisenhower's approval, Montgomery decided to try a very daring plan called Operation MARKET GARDEN.

The Allied First Airborne Army, stationed in southern England under American General Brereton, was placed under Montgomery's command. This army consisted of two American airborne divisions, one British airborne division, and a Polish airborne brigade. Montgomery planned to have the British 1st Airborne Division and the Polish brigade make a landing at Arnhem, in Holland, more than 60 miles from British front-line troops east of Antwerp. While the British and Polish paratroopers held the bridge over the Lek River, the British XXX Corps would drive northward through Belgium and Holland to link up with them and to cut off all German troops of the Fifteenth Army to the west. To help the British ground troops advance through the difficult network of canals and rivers between Arnhem and the British front, the American 82nd Airborne Division would land and seize the bridges over the Waal and Maas Rivers near Nijmegen, while the 101st Airborne Division would capture and hold bridges over the canals near Eindhoven.

The operation began on September 17. The British 1st Airborne Division landed a few miles from Arnhem, while the two American divisions dropped near their objectives. The Guards Armored Division fiercely spearheaded the northward drive of the British XXX Corps. The well-planned operation got off to an efficient start.

Things soon began to go wrong for the Allies, however. The weather turned bad; for five days supplies and follow-up forces could not be flown to Arnhem. When they landed in Arnhem, the British and the Poles discovered, to their surprise, that an additional German division was stationed there. This division quickly surrounded the British paratroopers who had seized the Lek Bridge, cutting the 1st Airborne Division into two separated groups. General Model and General Student — commander of the German First Parachute Army — were both near Arnhem, and they took immediate and personal charge of the German defense. They ordered bridges to be blown up and dikes blasted in the path of the advancing XXX Corps.

Both Germans and Allies fought gallantly and desperately. The two American divisions that held the key bridges at Nijmegen and Eindhoven suffered heavy losses against German counterattacks, while the British paratroopers held out against overwhelming odds in two small pockets near Arnhem. Their courageous defense was one of the great epics of British military history. But the XXX Corps could not get there in time to rescue them.

On September 21 the paratroopers at the Arnhem Bridge were forced to surrender. Next day a spearhead of the XXX Corps reached the south bank of the Lek River, but could not fight its way across. Three days later the pitiful remnants of the British 1st Airborne Division escaped to the south bank.

Operation MARKET GARDEN had not been a complete failure, but neither had it been a real success. A deep wedge had been driven into the German line, but that line had not been broken. German resistance was so fierce that the Allies could make no further advance in the flooded countryside. In their effort to open the port of Antwerp, the Allies further west had to continue their step-by-step advance along the Scheldt River and across the partly flooded Dutch islands.

Finally, in early November, after both sides had suffered great losses, the British gained complete control of the territory on both sides of the lower Scheldt River, but even then their work was not finished. German mines had to be swept from the channel of the river. It was November 28 before Allied ships were able to bring supplies into the port of Antwerp.

Slow Progress

FURTHER SOUTH, General Bradley's 12th Army Group, short of ammunition and other equipment, slowly battled its way forward. The American First Army, in a hard-fought battle beginning early in October, drove through the Siegfried Line near Aachen and on October 21, after eight days of street-fighting, captured the city. Meanwhile, the American Third Army had thrown back a German attack south of Metz. In early October it counterattacked, but by then the Germans were too well entrenched to be driven back easily. Allied advances were terribly slow.

By November the Americans had built up enough reserves of gasoline and ammunition to start some more attacks. A First Army drive through the Hurtgen Forest toward Cologne got off to a good start, but it was soon slowed down by German counterattacks ordered by General Model. A bitter battle for control of the forest continued into December, with the Allies making very little progress.

Further south, General Patton's Third Army had more spectacular success. The hard fight for Metz was finally ended on November 22, when the American troops surrounded the German defenders and forced them to surrender. By early December General Patton's men had reached the border of Germany north and east of Metz.

View from a gunport at Metz, France, showing tank obstacles in front of two wrecked American tanks.

Men of the Seventh American Army move through rain and mist to the attack.

In Alsace, General Devers' 6th Army Group was also making good progress. The American Seventh Army reached the German frontier along the Rhine River and further west. They captured Strasbourg on November 23, and held on to the city despite violent German counterattacks. At the same time the French First Army also reached the Rhine near the Swiss border, though the Germans still held on to a large portion of central Alsace around Colmar.

Allied advances in the fall of 1944 had been steady but unspectacular. After the great successes of July and August, the British and American people had had high hopes of an early end to the war in Europe, but it was now clear that there could be no Allied victory in 1944. The German army's recovery had been amazing. The skill and the ferocity of their defense was making some of the Allies wonder if they could be defeated even in 1945.

One thing that made the Germans fight harder was the announcement by Roosevelt and Churchill that they would insist on Germany's "unconditional surrender." By this the Allied leaders meant that they would not negotiate peace terms with Hitler's government, but would keep on fighting until Germany surrendered or was conquered. Hitler and his Nazis told the German people that this really meant that the Allies intended to destroy their country completely. Germany's only hope, they said, was to fight so hard that the Allies would get discouraged. The Nazis convinced the German soldiers that if they did not die fighting, they and their families would be killed or horribly mistreated after unconditional surrender.

Germany Strikes Back

The Buzz Bombs

BEFORE D-Day Hitler had warned the Allies that if they did not make peace he would use a "secret weapon" against them. Most people thought he was bluffing, but on June 12, less than a week after D-Day, a secret weapon really did come zooming across the

51

English Channel. It was the so-called "flying bomb" or "buzz bomb," the V-1 (*Vergeltungswaffe eins*, Vengeance Weapon one), which was actually a sort of pilotless jet plane. From hidden sites on the French coast the Germans launched the first of these powerful weapons against England. Three days later they sent 300 of them across the Channel. Most of them struck London, where they caused great damage. These "buzz bombs," flying at the speed of a very fast airplane, made enough noise to give a few seconds' warning of their arrival.

The citizens of London remained surprisingly calm as hundreds of these flying bombs rained destruction on their city, but Allied leaders were deeply concerned about the new weapons. The Royal Air Force, assisted by the American Eighth Air Force, immediately

American soldiers inspect German "buzz-bomb" site.

began bombing the V-1 launching sites. The Allied air strikes were not completely successful, for these sites were well protected by heavy concrete defenses. The V-1 attacks on London and southern England continued, though not so intensively. The fastest fighter planes of the Royal Air Force could sometimes intercept the V-1's in the air, and so the number of "buzz bombs" to reach London was kept under some control. Three thousand were fired during the five weeks following the first launching, but only 30 per cent penetrated the British defenses.

After the Allies broke out of the Normandy Beachhead, they soon cleared out the V-1 launching sites on the northern French coast. A few continued firing from the west coast of Holland, but this was so far away that only a few managed to cause much damage in England.

The V-2

MEANWHILE, Hitler was boasting of an even more terrible "secret weapon." Allied leaders soon learned from secret reports that again he was not bluffing. The first of these new secret weapons, the V-2 rocket, struck England on September 8, 1944. It had a much longer range than the V-1, and was successfully launched from Holland. This was the first of the rocket-propelled long-range missiles. It was propelled through the air at a rate much faster than the speed of sound, so that it arrived without warning. Its larger warhead was much more destructive than that of the V-1. The blows delivered by great numbers of these fearsome weapons soon began to shake even the stout spirits of the hardy British people.

At the same time that the Germans were battering England with the V-2's, they began to use these weapons — and the V-1's as well

53

— against the port of Antwerp, which the Allies had recently captured. When the seaport began to receive supply ships late in November, the Germans increased the intensity of the V-weapon attacks. By the time the last V-2 struck Antwerp — in March, 1945 — more than two-thirds of the city's buildings had been destroyed, and many thousands of Belgian civilians and Allied soldiers had been killed and wounded.

But Hitler was disappointed not only in his hope that the British people would insist upon peace in order to escape the attacks, but in his hope that the dock-workers of Antwerp would refuse to unload ships under the daily rain of death and destruction. He therefore decided to make one more great effort in the West.

Ardennes Offensive

REMEMBERING the great German victory of 1940 in the Ardennes region, the German dictator planned to have his armies make another drive through the same rugged country. They were to break through the Allied lines, seize the port of Antwerp, and destroy all Allied forces north of that city. Despite the terrible losses that Germany had suffered in the East and in the West, Hitler was convinced that the breakthrough could be made and a great victory won. He was confident that such a victory, combined with the rain of V-1 and V-2 bombs on England, would so discourage the Allies that they would make peace on terms favorable to Germany.

The German generals knew they could never completely defeat the powerful Allied armies, and they realized that one defeat would not cause the Allies to make peace. They obeyed their orders, however, and hoped that a German victory would make the Allies abandon their policy of unconditional surrender and bring the war to an end without too great disaster for Germany.

Field Marshal von Rundstedt was in over-all command of the Ardennes operation. "The Führer's fireman," General Model, in command of Army Group B, was directly responsible. The attack was to be made south of Aachen by the Sixth Panzer Army under SS General Sepp Dietrich, and the Fifth Panzer Army under General Hasso von Manteuffel. The striking force consisted of 24 divisions, ten of which were armored. These were the best troops of the German army, collected from east and west. All units were brought up to full strength. Dietrich's Sixth Panzer Army was to make the main effort. This was to be the same kind of *blitzkrieg* blow that had carried the Germans across Europe.

The area for attack had been chosen largely for the same reasons it had been chosen in 1940. It was rugged, forested, mountainous

Some of General Clark's men wait for German gunfire to cease before entering the captured town of St. Vith, Belgium.

country. Because it was so difficult to move large forces and fight in such country, the Ardennes was one portion of the Allied line where Allied units were spread thin. Also, since the Allies could not be strong everywhere, and since General Eisenhower was planning new and more important blows toward Cologne and into the Rhine-Moselle area further south, there were only weak forces holding the less important parts of the line.

The Germans knew that the Allied defenses were weak in this area, and hoped that the power of the German attack could get them through the difficult country before the Allies could delay them. The Germans, whose supply of gasoline and oil was too low to last more than a few days, knew that their chances of success lay in surprising and capturing Allied supply depots.

The Battle of the Bulge

IN THE FOGGY DAWN of December 16, the German attack swept forward on a 40-mile front. The Sixth Panzer Army in the north ran into four veteran American divisions of the VI Corps, and after a brief advance was stopped in its tracks. Further south, however, the Fifth Panzer Army, opposed on a 20-mile front by only two relatively inexperienced American divisions, made a breakthrough. Bad weather prevented American planes from helping the defending troops.

General Eisenhower rushed reinforcements to the front, but the German tanks and infantry continued to smash their way forward. One of the reinforcing divisions — the American 101st Airborne — and elements of other American units, were surrounded soon after they arrived at the Belgian town of Bastogne. By December 21 no one was quite sure where or when the Germans could be stopped.

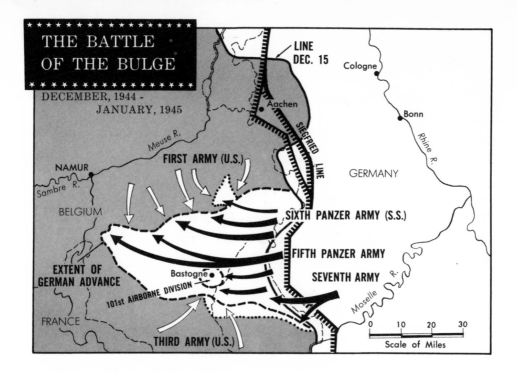

THE BATTLE
OF THE BULGE

DECEMBER, 1944 -
JANUARY, 1945

LINE
DEC. 15

Cologne

Aachen

Bonn

SIEGFRIED LINE

GERMANY

Rhine R.

Meuse R.

FIRST ARMY (U.S.)

NAMUR

Sambre R.

BELGIUM

SIXTH PANZER ARMY (S.S.)

FIFTH PANZER ARMY

EXTENT OF
GERMAN ADVANCE

Bastogne

SEVENTH ARMY

Moselle R.

101st AIRBORNE DIVISION

FRANCE

THIRD ARMY (U.S.)

0   10   20   30
Scale of Miles

Operations maps showed the German penetration as a huge bulge in the Allied lines. That is why some newspaper correspondents called this the "Battle of the Bulge."

To add to the confusion, it was now discovered that a number of English-speaking German SS soldiers in American uniforms were wandering around behind the Allied lines. Some had been dropped by parachute; others had taken advantage of Manteuffel's breakthrough to dash through the gap in captured American tanks, trucks and jeeps. These desperate men were supposed to create disorder in the Allied ranks by murdering high-ranking officers, cutting telephone and telegraph lines, and attacking American units from the rear. Rumors of such terror tactics created doubts and suspicions among American troops as far back as General Eisenhower's headquarters at Versailles near Paris.

Glaring newspaper headlines caused some panic in Britain and America, but there was little alarm among the fighting troops. Eisenhower and other Allied generals reacted coolly and efficiently. Veteran American divisions were still holding firm in their old positions north and south of the Bulge. Bradley and his corps commanders sent their reserves to hold the corners or "shoulders," of the German penetration in order to prevent the attackers from spreading out to widen the gap. The Germans tried vainly to push in these shoulders. They were thrown back with great losses.

Patton's tanks gather for the Bastogne attack.

With the base of the Bulge thus held to only about 35 miles, the Germans could not get enough room to maneuver their armored divisions in their favorite *blitzkrieg* fashion. All they could do was push straight ahead through the narrow gap. At the same time, American divisions were pulled out of the line north and south of the Bulge, and were rushing in to blunt and stop the German drive. The British XXX Corps — reserve of the 21st Army Group — was also moving in to help, if necessary. Meanwhile, the terror attacks by Germans in American uniform had accomplished nothing. Most of the imposters had been promptly captured by rear area units and military police.

On the German side, Model realized what was happening, and tried to shift two unused armored divisions from Dietrich's Sixth Panzer Army to Manteuffel's Fifth. He hoped to widen the gap before the American reserves closed in. But Dietrich was one of Hitler's favorites, and the German dictator wanted the SS general to get the main credit for the expected victory. He refused to let Model take any of Dietrich's armored divisions. A German victory at this time had been distinctly unlikely from the beginning. Hitler's stubbornness made it impossible.

Meanwhile, the American stronghold at Bastogne had blocked one of the main roads that the Germans were using, and so General von Manteuffel made every effort to overwhelm the American garrison. Assembling large forces around the town, he called upon the defenders to surrender. But Brigadier General Anthony McAuliffe, commanding the 101st Airborne Division, replied to the surrender demand with one contemptuous word: "Nuts!" While American aircraft dropped supplies of food and ammunition to the surrounded troops, McAuliffe's men beat off every German attack.

Unable to take Bastogne, and unable to reach any large American fuel supply depots, the Germans began to run out of gasoline. On December 24 their spearhead tanks were stopped four miles from the Meuse River by American and British units. This was the furthest extent of "the Bulge."

While these events were taking place, the American Third Army had called off an attack which it had just started further to the south. General Patton shifted his divisions, and on December 22 struck a powerful blow against the south flank of the Bulge. As the weather improved, American fighter and bomber planes joined in the attack, smashing German positions in and behind the Bulge. The day after Christmas one of Patton's armored divisions drove through ice and snow to break the German lines around the 101st Division. What little chance of success the German offensive had had ended when the siege of Bastogne was broken.

The battle continued with undiminished intensity. Now, however, it was the Americans — joined by a few British units in the north — who were attacking, and the Germans who were trying grimly to hold on to what they had won. But the outcome was never in doubt. The exhausted German soldiers, brave and determined though they were, now realized that they could never win the war, and that the losses they had taken in trying to push through the Ardennes could never be replaced. Slowly the defenders fell back, fighting fiercely to hold on to every inch of ground. By January 16, after a month of terribly bloody fighting, the Germans were almost back where they had started; the Bulge had disappeared.

The results of Hitler's Ardennes offensive had been even worse than his generals had feared. Although it had delayed Eisenhower's planned drive into Germany by about six weeks, it had resulted in more than 200,000 German casualties, while the Americans had lost less than half that number. German supplies, too, had been wasted, and that meant that when the Russians and the Western Allies began their attacks, both would be able to advance much more rapidly.

To the Rhine and Over

Hitler Makes Another Mistake

THE ARDENNES OFFENSIVE, instead of improving the German situation, had actually made it worse. The best units of the German army had been badly battered, and the losses could never be replaced.

Bastogne. Bomb-wrecked buildings.

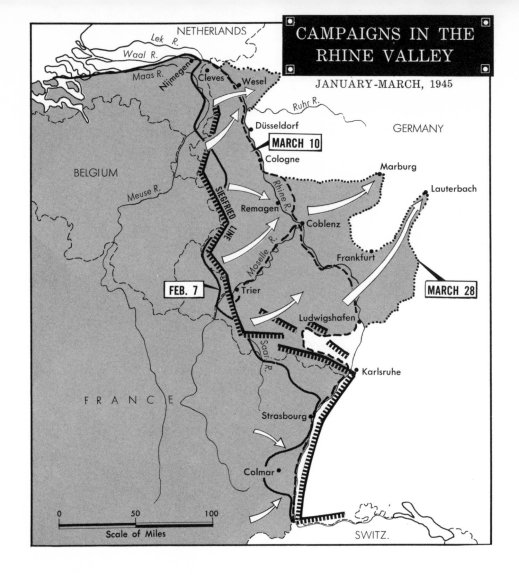

NETHERLANDS

Lek R.

Waal R.

Maas R.

Nijmegen

Cleves

Wesel

Ruhr R.

Düsseldorf

MARCH 10

GERMANY

Cologne

Marburg

BELGIUM

Meuse R.

SIEGFRIED LINE

Remagen

Rhine R.

Lauterbach

Coblenz

Moselle R.

Frankfurt

FEB. 7

Trier

MARCH 28

Saar R.

Ludwigshafen

Karlsruhe

FRANCE

Strasbourg

Colmar

0   50   100

Scale of Miles

SWITZ.

Neither was it possible to replace the great quantities of gasoline
burned by the German tanks as they tried to drive through the Bulge.

Hitler should have realized that the Allies now had more troops
than he, and that these troops were better supplied and in better
condition than his own. But in early January, instead of holding
back his few remaining reserves, he ordered another offensive. This

62

time it was in northern Alsace, where some American units had been pulled out of the line to take part in the Battle of the Bulge.

Hitler's generals knew that the temporary weakening of the American line would make it possible for them to advance for a short time. But they were also aware of the weaknesses of their own armies. They realized that Germany's chances for success were even slimmer than they had been in the Ardennes. They protested to Hitler, but he ordered the attack nevertheless.

As the German generals had expected, they were able to move ahead for a while. They briefly threatened Allied control of Strasbourg, but in less than two weeks they were halted completely by the arrival of more American troops. On January 20, the French and Americans began a powerful counterblow against the German pocket of resistance at Colmar in southern Alsace. By February 9, they had driven the Germans across the Rhine.

Meanwhile, General Eisenhower was completing his plans for a new, massive offensive. Realizing that the Germans were now dangerously short of trained troops and supplies, he made certain that they had no time to rest. While the Franco-American drive continued in southern Alsace, the American First and Third armies conducted limited offensives in the Ardennes region, and the British Second Army made similar attacks along the lower Roer River.

The first great Allied offensive of 1945 began on February 8 with a concerted drive against the Siegfried Line. The front stretched from Cleves, in the north, to Trier, on the Moselle River. The main effort was made on the left by Montgomery's 21st Army Group, now consisting of General Crerar's Canadian First, General Dempsey's British Second, and General Simpson's American Ninth armies. The Germans resisted fiercely, but the Allies pushed steadily ahead. Within four weeks they had advanced to the left bank of

La Roche, France. United States troops hunt for German snipers.

the Rhine River from Nijmegen, in eastern Netherlands, almost to Cologne, though the Germans still retained a few footholds on the west side of the river. At the same time General Bradley's 12th Army Group, still consisting of Hodge's First and Patton's Third armies, had pushed through the Siegfried Line north and south of the Moselle River.

The Rhineland Campaign

ON MARCH 6, the armored divisions of General Bradley's two armies smashed their way through the northern Rhineland to the Rhine and Moselle rivers. So rapid was their advance that the Germans did not have time to blow up the railroad bridge over the Rhine at Remagen before it was seized on March 7 by the American 9th Armored Division. General Bradley and General Hodges rushed reinforcements to establish a bridgehead on the east bank of the Rhine opposite Remagen, and repulsed all German attempts to drive them back. By March 10, both American armies were firmly established not only at the Remagen Bridgehead on the right bank of the Rhine, but all along the left bank, too. They had overrun more than 3,000 square miles of Germany in less than four days.

The Americans did not halt for an instant. While General Hodges poured First Army troops across the Rhine to strengthen and enlarge the Remagen Bridgehead, General Patton's Third Army turned southeast to join the Seventh Army of General Devers' 6th Army Group in a sweep through the Rhineland country southeast of the Moselle River. In ten days — March 11 to March 21 — the Third Army slashed through the Hunsruck Mountains and along the left bank of the Rhine River to conquer the region between Coblenz and Ludwigshafen. General Patch's American Seventh Army advanced more slowly because it was hindered by the Siegfried Line defenses in the Saar River region.

By March 21, the Germans held only one important foothold on the left bank of the Rhine River in the region just west of Karlsruhe. In their two weeks of slashing assaults through the Rhineland the three American armies had captured about 250,000 prisoners, and had killed or wounded 60-100,000 Germans. At the same time, the

Anti-aircraft batteries guard Allied troops crossing the Remagen bridge over the Rhine.

Americans had lost about 15,000 men killed and wounded. The German Army of the West had been smashed beyond repair. Yet, surprisingly, the Germans fought on.

The Rhine Crossings

Now GENERAL EISENHOWER was ready for his final offensive into Germany. Montgomery's 21st Army Group would carry the heaviest weight of the assault. His three armies would cross the Rhine north of the Ruhr River, then sweep eastward across the north German plain. Eisenhower expected that the war would end when units of the 21st Army Group reached Berlin or made contact with the Russians near the German capital. Since most of the Allied supplies would go to Montgomery, General Bradley's 12th Army Group and General Devers' 6th Army Group were only expected to keep the Germans too busy to interfere with the great assault. General Eisenhower did not intend that these two groups should make any more spectacular drives such as they had carried out in the Rhineland.

While First Army troops pour across the Rhine Bridge, Nazi prisoners stream west to internment.

Montgomery's grand attack was to get started on March 23 with a river-crossing over the Rhine near Wesel. The British general had been carefully preparing for that attack during the two weeks when the American First, Third, and Seventh armies had been fighting in the Rhineland further south.

Most of the American generals did not agree with General Eisenhower's plan to have Montgomery's army group make the main attack. They felt that their American armies should have an important part in the final defeat of Germany. For this reason, General Bradley planned to have Hodges' First Army make as strong an attack from the Remagen Bridgehead as the limited Allied supplies would permit.

Then suddenly, on March 22, just one day before Montgomery was scheduled to cross, General Patton made a full-scale assault over the Rhine River at Oppenheim. It came as a surprise not only to the Germans but to most of the Allies. Although Patton's Third Army had been marching and fighting steadily for more than a month, Patton had planned carefully for this attack, and his divisions assembled quickly for the crossing. General Patton made this river-crossing without orders, but he was not being disobedient. He had never been told he should not cross the Rhine.

The following day the British Second and American Ninth armies crossed the Rhine at Wesel, in Montgomery's carefully planned, well-conducted attack. They were opposed by considerably larger and better prepared German forces than those Patton had brushed aside. Nevertheless, the British and American soldiers soon had themselves established on the east bank of the Rhine, and on March 25 Montgomery started a full-scale sweep into the North German plain. On that same day Hodges' First Army broke out of the Remagen Bridgehead, and by March 28 three major Allied spearheads were sweeping deep into Central Germany.

Through Eastern Europe to Berlin

The Baltic and the Balkans

BY THE FALL OF 1944 the German armies had been stretched so thin on the Eastern Front that even Hitler realized there was no hope unless they withdrew to establish a new, shorter line. In September, therefore, he had told General Guderian to go ahead with his plan to pull back and regroup the shattered German armies.

To gain time and space to make an orderly withdrawal, Guderian ordered a counterattack in Latvia in mid-September. It was successful, and the Germans began to pull back. Then suddenly Hitler ordered the troops to stay where they were, completely ruining Guderian's plan.

In October the Russians took advantage of the situation. They moved forces north and started another great offensive in Latvia and the other Baltic States. Quickly they broke through to the Baltic Sea, cutting off all German forces in northern Latvia and Estonia. Then in late October the Russians suddenly shifted their reserves and attacked into Lithuania and East Prussia. A violent German counterattack soon brought them to a halt, but for the first time in the war, Russian troops had reached German soil.

Again Stalin turned his attention to southern Europe. His troops quickly broke through the thin German screen in the mountains of western Romania and western Bulgaria, and streamed into Hungary and Yugoslavia. Belgrade fell on October 20.

The Russians quickly made contact with the Yugoslav Resistance forces who had been holding out successfully against the Germans for three years in the mountainous areas of Yugoslavia. These guerrilla fighters, commanded by the dedicated Communist, Josip Broz

Tito, were inspired partly by patriotism and partly by Communist anti-German propaganda. Though the fighters had received more supplies by air-drop from the British and Americans than they had from the Russians, their leader, Tito, immediately established a pro-Russian Communist puppet government over Yugoslavia.

The Russians continued to advance without a break. By October 29 they had reached the outskirts of Budapest, capital of Hungary. Here German resistance stiffened, and a bitter battle began in and around Budapest. By November 24 the Russians had succeeded in forcing a crossing over the Danube south of the city, but it was another month before they managed to encircle the Hungarian capital.

The Germans outside of Budapest counterattacked, and almost broke through to the city. The Russians kept their hold around the city, but they failed to dislodge the stubborn Germans inside it. Since Budapest controlled the Danube Valley and all the main roads and railroad lines toward Austria and Germany, the Russians could advance no farther. The great battle for Budapest continued for another six weeks. Finally, on February 13, 1945, the Russians captured the last German stronghold in the city. The road to Vienna was now open. The Russian steamroller began to move again in the Danube Valley.

Poland, Germany, and Austria

WHILE THE STRUGGLE for Budapest was going on, Stalin had ordered his generals to renew the offensive in Poland and East Prussia. The Russian armies in this region probably made up the largest military force ever gathered together on the continent of Europe. But by this time Hitler had moved all of his reserves and all of his best troops to the west to take part in the Ardennes Offensive. When the Rus-

70

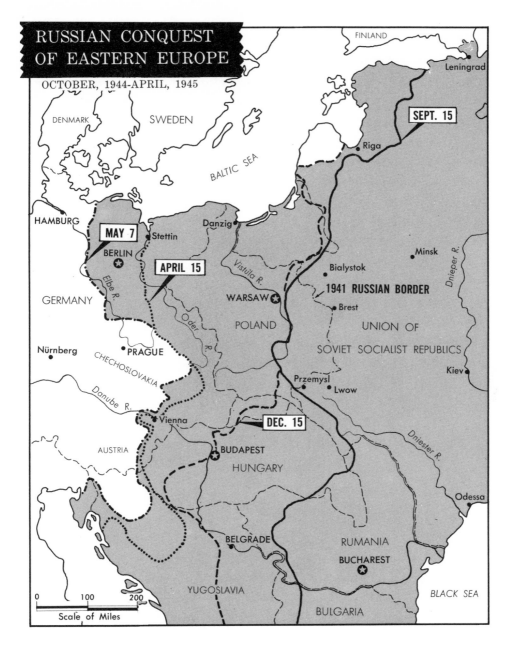

RUSSIAN CONQUEST
OF EASTERN EUROPE

OCTOBER, 1944-APRIL, 1945

FINLAND

DENMARK

SWEDEN

Leningrad

SEPT. 15

BALTIC SEA

Riga

HAMBURG

MAY 7

Stettin

Danzig

Minsk

Dnieper R.

BERLIN

APRIL 15

Vistula R.

Bialystok

1941 RUSSIAN BORDER

GERMANY

Elbe R.

Oder R.

WARSAW

Brest

UNION OF

Nürnberg

PRAGUE

CHECHOSLOVAKIA

POLAND

SOVIET SOCIALIST REPUBLICS

Kiev

Danube R.

Przemysl

Lwow

Dniester R.

DEC. 15

Vienna

AUSTRIA

BUDAPEST

HUNGARY

Odessa

BELGRADE

RUMANIA

BUCHAREST

0   100   200

Scale of Miles

YUGOSLAVIA

BULGARIA

BLACK SEA

71

sians struck in Poland on January 12, 1945, they outnumbered the Germans more than ten-to-one. In a month's time they swept over Poland and reached the line of the Oder River, a mere 30 miles from Berlin. Here the Germans resisted so fanatically that they completely halted the Russian advance.

Unable to move farther westward, the Russians turned north and overran East Prussia. On March 30 they captured Danzig after a terribly bloody battle. Two weeks later they wiped out the last important German strongholds in East Prussia. But the Germans repulsed their every effort to drive on to Berlin.

Once more Stalin increased his pressure against the German southern flank. Hitler had ordered a counterattack against Budapest in March, but the Russians had stopped it. It was the German Army's last important offensive. Now the Russians pushed ahead almost without resistance. By April 13 they had captured Vienna.

Hitler's Germany had not the slightest chance to survive much longer. Yet, amazingly, the Germans still held grimly to the line of the Oder River in mid-April.

The Fall of Germany

Ruhr Encirclement

IN THE LAST DAYS of March, 1945, the Western Allies gained momentum as they fanned out over the area east of the Rhine River. To the north, in Montgomery's 21st Army Group, the Canadian First Army swung northwestward into Holland; armored units of the British Second Army swept northeastward toward Hamburg; the American Ninth Army drove due east toward the Weser River.

The most spectacular advances were made by the American armored units of the Ninth Army, in Montgomery's group, and by the First and Third armies in Bradley's group. On April 1 the spearheads of General Simpson's Ninth Army and General Hodges' First met near Paderborn, in west central Germany. General Model's Army Group B was encircled in an area of some 4,000 square miles.

Model had about 500,000 men, well supplied with food and ammunition. He defended the vital Ruhr industrial region skillfully, and despite Hitler's orders not to give up an inch of German territory, made plans to fight his way out of the trap.

But the Americans had no intention of allowing any of the encircled Germans to escape. While the armored spearheads continued to drive east into central Germany, other divisions of the Ninth and First armies smashed against Model's defensive lines. Skillful and determined as they were, the Germans could not stop the equally skillful and determined Americans. By April 14 the Americans had split Model's army group into two parts. On the same day Hitler radioed Model to try to break out of the trap.

The German general realized that it was hopeless to resist any longer. Refusing to be responsible for the loss of any more German lives, he disbanded his armies and then committed suicide. By April 18 the last of his command had surrendered. The Allies took a total of 317,000 prisoners. At least 150,000 more of Model's troops had simply dropped their weapons, changed their clothes, and disappeared into the civilian population.

Drive to the Elbe

MEANWHILE, the Allied advance eastward through Germany continued. On April 18 advance units of the Ninth Army had reached

American troops search German prisoners for hidden weapons.

the line of the Elbe River on a broad front, and one unit had actually seized a bridgehead east of the river. On the same day, having encircled the German Eleventh Army in the Harz Mountains, the spearheads of the First Army had reached Leipzig and the Mulde

River. At the same time the Third Army, undismayed by the mountainous Thuringian Forest, had captured Hof on the frontier of Czechoslovakia. Units of the American Seventh Army were in the outskirts of Nurnberg. Others — along with troops of the French First Army — were approaching Stuttgart. In the north the Canadians were clearing Holland, while the British Second Army was

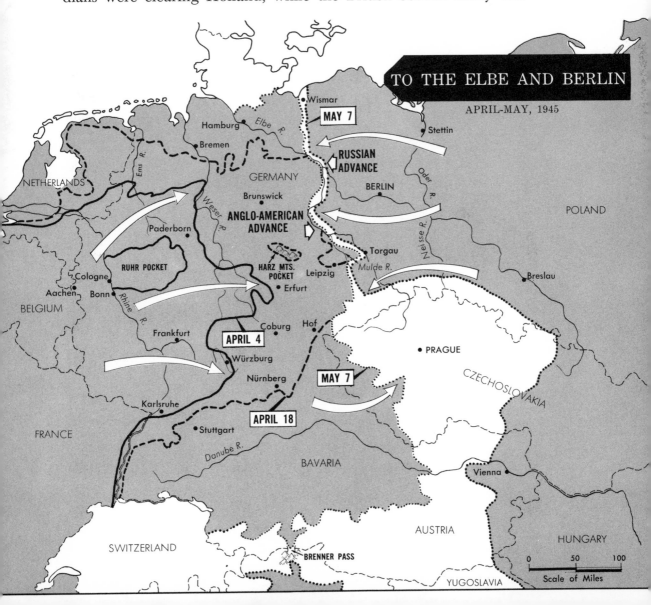

TO THE ELBE AND BERLIN

APRIL-MAY, 1945

approaching Hamburg and the lower Elbe River.

The Western Allies were now almost as close to Berlin as were the Russians. But the Russians were still opposed by strong and effective armies, while German forces in the West had practically collapsed. General Eisenhower was now urged by some of his subordinates — particularly by Montgomery — to continue the advance to Berlin. It would have taken the British or American armored divisions no more than two days to reach the German capital. Prime Minister Churchill of Britain also urged Eisenhower to keep on going.

But General Eisenhower, guided by the American Joint Chiefs of Staff, believed that there were military tasks more important than beating the Russians to Berlin. He was worried by rumors of last-ditch German resistance fighters in the mountains of southeastern Germany. Also, the Allied civilian leaders — Roosevelt, Churchill, and Stalin — had agreed on occupation zones in Germany once Hitler's government collapsed. British and American troops were already deep in the Russian area, and would have to be withdrawn once the fighting was over. It was obvious that the Russians could capture Berlin without American or British help. Eisenhower thought that it would be best to use his armies to prevent any collection of German resistance fighters in Bavaria, Austria, or Czechoslovakia.

Eisenhower, therefore, held the Ninth and First armies on the line of the Elbe and Mulde Rivers. Montgomery was not permitted to advance to Berlin, but was limited to completing the occupation of north-central Germany. Meanwhile, Patton's Third Army was allowed to slash its way down the Danube Valley and across the mountains into Czechoslovakia, while Devers' group continued its advance to the line of the Alps and the Brenner Pass.

Tanks of the United States Third Army enter Cologne.

The Fall of Berlin

BEFORE the collapse of the Western Front, the Germans had repulsed every Russian attempt to drive across the Oder River to Berlin. During early April, however, Stalin concentrated a tremendous force between Stettin and Breslau in preparation for a final blow against Germany. Approximately eight armies were massed in this small area. They were organized into two great army groups: the

First White Russian Group, commanded by Marshal Vasily D. Soko-
lovski, and the First Ukrainian Group, under Marshal Ivan S. Konev.
Russia's leading general, Marshal Georgi K. Zhukov, was in over-all
command.

During the night of April 16-17, the Russians struck. Not even the
most fanatical Nazi — not even Hitler himself — had any hope of stop-
ping the massive Russian offensive. But Hitler and his henchmen
knew that if they surrendered they would be treated as the murder-
ous war criminals they were. By keeping the specter of unconditional surrender constantly before the eyes of the German people,
Hitler persuaded them to fight to the bitter end. Even though the
Americans and British were advancing rapidly in the west, the
terribly outnumbered German forces along the Oder fought desperately to stem the Russian advance. So it was that it took the
Russians six days to smash their way 30 miles to the outskirts of
Berlin. Three days later, on April 25, spearheads of Zhukov's armies
met west of Berlin to cut off the German capital from the limited
area of Germany still under Nazi control.

Hitler himself had stayed in Berlin to take personal command of
the German soldiers there. He ordered them to fight to the last man.
With no thought for his people, he had decided to die in a terrible
last battle that would bring his country and his capital down in final
ruin with him.

During the whole war there was no more bitter fighting than that
which now took place in Berlin. It raged from street to street, from
house to house. On April 30, Hitler committed suicide. On May 2,
the last German defending soldier was killed or captured.

Enraged by the fierce resistance of the Germans, eager to get re-
venge for German outrages in Russia, and attracted by the remaining
riches in the shattered city, Russian soldiers roamed through the

streets, looting, killing German civilian men, and terribly mistreating the German women. The people of Berlin were learning what had happened earlier to the cities Hitler had conquered.

The End of the War

DURING the battle for Berlin, other Russian units had continued westward to meet the Western Allies. The British and American troops had been waiting for several days on a line running generally south from Wismar, and then along the Elbe River to the border of Czechoslovakia. The Russians made their first contact with these British and American troops at Torgau, on the Elbe, on April 25, but it was another week before the Russians had moved up all along the line. On May 2, at the request of the Russians, General Eisenhower ordered Patton to stop his advance into Czechoslovakia.

Those German troops that still remained in organized formations had begun to surrender to the Western Allies even before the fall of Berlin. Now the surrenders became general. On May 5 most German forces in Holland, Denmark, and northern Germany surrendered, and so, the next day, did Army Group G, in southern Germany.

At this time, Admiral Karl Doenitz, who was in northern Germany and who had been named by Hitler as his successor, began to negotiate for the final surrender of Germany and of all remaining German land, sea, and air forces. The surrender took place in the French city of Reims, May 7, 1945.

VE day — victory in Europe — was celebrated with great rejoicing in every Allied country, but there was little time for rejoicing by Allied forces in the Pacific and in Asia. They were still fighting a war against Japan.

Index

81